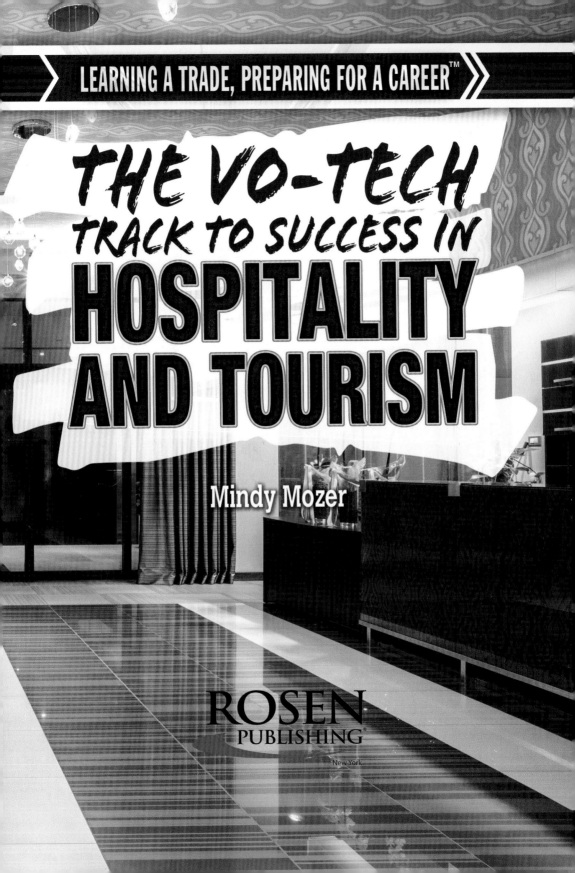

LEARNING A TRADE, PREPARING FOR A CAREER™

THE VO-TECH
TRACK TO SUCCESS IN
HOSPITALITY AND TOURISM

Mindy Mozer

ROSEN
PUBLISHING

New York

…sen Publishing Group, Inc.
…k, NY 10010

…sen Publishing Group, Inc.

First Edition.

Library of Congress Cataloging-in-Publication Data

Mozer, Mindy.
The Vo-Tech track to success in hospitality and tourism/Mindy Mozer.
    pages cm. — (Learning a trade, preparing for a career)
Includes bibliographical references and index.
Audience: Grades 7-12.
ISBN 978-1-4777-7728-2 (library bound)
1. Hospitality industry—Vocational guidance—Juvenile literature.
2. Tourism—Vocational guidance—Juvenile literature. I. Title.
TX911.3.V62M69 2015
338.4'791—dc23

                             2014001774

Manufactured in the United States of America

CONTENTS

The event planner was nervous. She was organizing a party for a celebrity in a five-star hotel, and everything had to be perfect. The head chef was doing his part, making sure that the food was cooked perfectly, looked beautiful on the plate, and lived up to the restaurant's five-star rating—the top rating available. The waiters and waitresses had to serve the food in a professional way, not spilling a drop.

The hotel manager had her workers on high alert. Every need of the guests had to be met. Check-in needed to be quick for those spending the night, and the rooms had to be spotless.

The party room had to look glamorous, fitting for this celebrity-studded special event. After all, photos of the event were going to be tweeted and put on Facebook and Instagram. Coverage was also likely to appear in celebrity news magazines. The night could be spoiled even if one employee didn't do his or her job correctly.

Welcome to the world of hospitality and tourism. Although not every event is this glamorous, jobs in the field can be exciting and rewarding—and many can be attained without a college education.

Vocational training is a path that many students choose to take on their way to a career in hospitality and tourism. A vo-tech education, as it is called, teaches

A housekeeping manager makes sure hotel rooms are clean and tidy before guests arrive. First impressions are important in the hospitality field.

employable skills in a variety of fields. The emphasis of such programs—which are offered by trade organizations, community colleges, private institutions, and even some high schools—is on practical career training, rather than general learning as it occurs in most four-year colleges.

The hospitality and tourism career path lends itself well to vo-tech training. The field is big and has room for people with different educational backgrounds. That includes those with a high school diploma, an associate's degree from a community college, or a vocational certificate, as well as those who opt for a four-year college degree. The field consists of every member of a kitchen staff, from head chefs to prep cooks, and every member of a hotel, resort, or cruise ship staff. Travel agents who plan business trips and vacations are part of the hospitality industry, as are recreation directors at summer camps. Some of these workers, such as event planners, are managers who oversee operations. Others are employees responsible for a small area of each customer's visit.

Students interested in hospitality and tourism can jump-start their careers in high school by taking vo-tech classes in restaurant management, food services, lodging, travel, and tourism. High schools may also partner with community colleges to offer programs in the hospitality and tourism fields, allowing students to receive college credit while still in high school. Some students are able to obtain internships at hotels and restaurants, giving them the experience they need to land a job after graduation.

Hospitality work can be rewarding when a high-level event runs smoothly or a family who has been planning a "trip of a lifetime" has a good time. Anyone who likes to travel and work with people should read on, even if not planning on going to college. A career in hospitality and tourism may be in your future.

Chapter One

RECIPE FOR SUCCESS

Working in the restaurant, beverage, and food service industry can be exciting. Think about it: there are job opportunities wherever people eat. That means not only restaurants, but also cruise ships, hotels, casinos, college campuses, resorts, nursing homes, hospitals, airports, daycare centers, and schools.

In the Kitchen

There are many different levels of staff in a professional kitchen. These include various types of chefs and cooks.

Executive chefs and head cooks are the people who make sure that everything runs smoothly. They work with the kitchen staff to properly prepare the food, make it tasty, and serve it on time to guests. Executive chefs may come up with the menu, help purchase ingredients, and train others in the kitchen.

Sous chefs are the chefs' assistants and are usually second-in-command of the kitchen. *Sous* means

Professional kitchens hire many different kinds of chefs, who all work together to prepare meals that keep customers coming back to their restaurant or business.

"underneath" in French, as in "under the chef." Sous chefs are middle managers. They supervise cooks and report to the head chef.

Prep cooks help chefs prepare meals. They do this by chopping vegetables, making salads, and putting food onto plates. Also known as line cooks, prep cooks may also help keep the kitchen clean by taking out the trash and washing dishes. Prep cooks may even deliver dishes to customers, depending on the restaurant. In some kitchens, a prep cook may work on only one part of dinner, such as salads or desserts.

Personal chefs work in private homes. These chefs may be self-employed or work for a company that places chefs in homes. Private chefs, for example, might work for company executives who routinely have people over for dinner.

Duties and Responsibilities

The job description for chefs of all types revolves around food. First and foremost is that chefs and cooks prepare food: chopping, mixing, stirring, sautéing, etc. Making sure that the food being prepared, and all other necessary ingredients, are fresh is an important part of the process.

Ensuring that there are enough fresh ingredients so that food can be prepared is the job of head chefs. This requires planning, ordering, and checking inventory. Speaking of menus, head chefs are also responsible for creating the list of dishes being served, as well as experimenting and creating new recipes to please customers.

As the title implies, head chefs are in charge of coordinating all food preparation activities by overseeing the work of other chefs and cooks in the kitchen. Even something like the size of food portions or the presentation of food on the plate is typically dictated by the head chef. Hiring and training other chefs and food prep workers also falls under the job duties of head chefs.

Ensuring that the kitchen is clean and meets health code standards, and that workers under his or her supervision handle food properly, fall to the head chef as well.

Work Environment

According to the Bureau of Labor Statistics' *Occupational Outlook Handbook*, almost half of all chefs work in full-service restaurants. But chefs can be found anywhere food is served. That means hotels, private households, cruise ships, casinos, school cafeterias, nursing homes, and even fast-food restaurants.

The work a chef does can be challenging. Kitchens are often hot because the ovens are on, and they can be crowded with workers. People working in kitchens also need to be careful because there are many ways to get injured. A chef can slip, get burned, or cut a finger while slicing. Kitchen injuries are usually minor, though.

Most chefs work full-time, but the hours can be challenging. Some work early mornings or late evenings to prepare food for busy dining times. Chefs often work weekends and holidays. Head chefs may

A culinary arts professor demonstrates a technique at a community college in Colorado. Many community colleges offer certification programs in cooking and food preparation.

work long days because they have to be there early to oversee the delivery of food, plan the menu, and complete other administrative tasks.

Education and Training

Most cooks learn on the job, perhaps starting their careers by working in kitchens in lower-level positions,

FOOD ON THE GO

Food trucks are the latest trend in large and small cities. These are mobile kitchens that sell food at festivals, farmers' markets, carnivals, college campuses, and other special events. Some are stationed in business districts. They are like ice cream trucks but with lunch and dinner options. Food trucks usually specialize in a certain type of food, such as Mexican food, hamburgers and hot dogs, or barbeque. Food truck owners hire chefs and servers, just like regular restaurants. Some chefs may buy their own food trucks and operate them as their own business.

such as line cooks or even dishwashers. Others move up the ranks through an apprenticeship, which is a situation wherein students learn by working under a professional in a given field.

Professional chefs, on the other hand, usually attend school for formal training. Chefs and head chefs who want formal vo-tech training may find that enrolling in a culinary arts certification program is the right fit for them. Courses cover such topics as food safety, menu planning, and basic nutrition. A certificate program typically takes one year to complete.

Organizations such as the American Culinary Federation offer certifications for many different levels of chefs, including sous chef, master chef, and executive chef. High school graduates can earn certification by working in a professional kitchen for a set number of years (between two and five years, depending on the level of chef that one aspires to) and passing written and practical exams. Practical exams mean that a student performs the duties of a chef in front of a panel of judges or teachers.

Some community colleges, which grant two-year associate's degrees, offer formal culinary programs. Along with culinary classes, students fulfill general education requirements, such as writing and business classes. Students who want bachelor's degrees can enroll in hospitality management programs at four-year colleges and universities. Along with learning about culinary techniques, students take classes in business and management, as well as electives.

Some chefs participate in formal apprenticeship programs sponsored by professional culinary institutes, industry associations, and trade unions. These programs combine classroom training and work experience. The American Culinary Federation offers two-year and three-year apprenticeship programs. Once the program is completed, apprentice graduates are eligible to test for the Certified Culinarian (CC) or Certified Pastry Culinarian (CPC) designation.

Chefs and cooks with experience will have the easiest time getting work. The long hours and fast pace of the job frequently lead to high turnover in the field.

Bakers

Bakers can be found in restaurants, grocery stores, manufacturing facilities, and, of course, bakeries.

Bakers prepare different types of baked goods, such as breads and pastries. Commercial bakers work in manufacturing facilities, where they make large quantities of baked goods that are then served in restaurants or sold in stores. Retail bakers work in grocery stores and specialty shops. Retail bakers take orders, prepare baked goods, and may even serve customers. Some retail bakers own their own bakeries.

Job Duties

Put simply, bakers bake. This involves many obvious tasks, such as gathering and measuring ingredients, combining them, leaving them in ovens to bake, and putting any finishing touches on their goods. Seems simple enough, like something many people manage to do in their own homes every day. The difference is that professional bakers do all this in volume. Baking in bulk, and doing so every day for freshness, requires planning and expert time management.

Another difference between professional bakers and home bakers is that the former use professional-grade commercial equipment. Depending on the size of the bakery or restaurant, or how many places that a commercial baker supplies, the heavy-duty equipment can include mixers, fryers, and ovens. Professional bakers need to be comfortable using such items, and that usually requires training.

Like chefs, bakers create recipes to please the palates of customers. Creating unique, tasty pastries and breads is one way that bakers can help their businesses, and the businesses they supply, differentiate themselves from the competition. That is part of running a business, which is what head bakers and bakery owners must do.

Work Environment

Most bakers work in bakeries, grocery stores, or restaurants. Bakers can work in resorts and hotels,

A young baker presents bread fresh out of the oven. Students who want to bake can learn how through community college and vocational school programs.

on cruise ships and college campuses, and with catering companies. Bakers can be found in small family-owned bakeries and large corporate operations.

Like chefs, bakers work in hot kitchens that can be noisy. They also work on deadline because they have to have items done at certain times. Some work late evenings or early-morning shifts to make sure that baked goods are ready for the breakfast crowd. Bakers work weekends and holidays because people eat pastries on the weekends, too.

Bakers have to stand for long periods of time and lift heavy bags, such as those filled with flour. They also work near hot ovens, so they're at risk of getting minor burns.

Education and Training

Like chefs, bakers may start as apprentices or assistants and learn on the job. Community colleges and vocational schools offer culinary classes that focus on baking. Bakers with specialized skills and experience will have the easiest time finding work—a fact that makes the case for bakers obtaining training and certification.

Bakers can get certified through the Retail Bakers of America (RBA). The RBA provides four certifications: Certified Journey Baker (CJB), Certified Baker (CB), Certified Decorator (CD), and Certified Master Baker (CMB). The amount of education and experience needed is different for each certification. For instance, there is no education requirement for a CJB, the first level of certification. But this certification requires at least one year of experience. A CMB must have completed a sanitation course, thirty hours of professional development courses, and eight years of work experience.

Wait Staff

Waiters and waitresses are the bridge between the chefs and the customers. Without them, customers wouldn't get their food. Also called servers, wait staff can be found in restaurants, airports, cruise ships, hotels, casinos, office cafeterias, nightclubs—essentially anywhere food is served.

Job Duties

Wait staff are the face of a restaurant or other food service facility. They are the people who have the most frequent interaction with customers, which puts the need to have strong people skills at the top of their job requirements list. Many upscale establishments employ a maître d' who greets and seats diners, while other restaurants might have a host or hostess who performs the same function. Yet in many smaller or chain food-service businesses, wait staff welcome customers and make sure that they find a table.

Simply handing people a menu and taking their order is the very least that wait staff are expected to do as part of their job. Professional waiters and waitresses who take their jobs seriously are also salespeople and a source of information. Familiarity with the menu is incredibly important, since wait staff will need to answer questions about specials, which change every day, as well as how a dish is prepared and what ingredients are used. For example, customers may want to know if items on the menu are gluten-free or lactose-free.

Waiters and waitresses may need to "push," or try to get customers to order certain items on the menu, so that a restaurant doesn't get stuck with extra food that will go bad. This may require meeting with the chef at the beginning of each shift. They also need to be good at trying to sell extras, such as appetizers and desserts, so that the restaurant can make more money.

Wait staff communicate with kitchen employees about what has been ordered, and they deliver orders to customers once they are fulfilled. Some wait staff are responsible for pouring soft drinks and other nonalcoholic beverages for customers. Depending on whether or not an establishment has hired bussers, whose job it is to clear tables, wait staff may also be responsible for removing dirty dishes and cleaning tables, as well as preparing tables for the next customers. Finally, waiters and waitresses tabulate the amount owed and see to it that payment is made for services offered.

Work Environment

Waiters and waitresses stand for long periods of time. They carry heavy trays of food. Their job can be stressful at busy times because customers expect good service. Most servers work part-time. Many work evenings, weekends, and holidays. Like kitchen staff, waiters and

Among the requirements for food servers is the ability to carry and balance heavy trays loaded with food and dining implements, while preserving the presentation of dishes as well.

waitresses work in any place where food is served, from cruise ships to high-end restaurants to family diners. Some may work in resorts for just a few months a year.

Education and Training

Waiters and waitresses learn on the job. They may learn about food safety from new employee training programs. In addition, new employees may shadow more experienced employees to learn serving techniques and communication skills. No formal education is required to enter this occupation. However, education programs are available for students wishing to receive training in the restaurant business.

The National Restaurant Association's Education Foundation operates ProStart, a two-year course of study for high school students interested in a restaurant career. The program is a mix of classes that teach restaurant and food service skills with actual work experience, learning on the job under the supervision of a mentor. Classes offered through the program do have a management focus. But other skills that would be valuable for wait staff, such as kitchen essentials, safety and sanitation, and customer service, are part of the program as well. Besides, it wouldn't hurt students to have management training in case they decide to work their way into a management position later in their careers.

Participants in the ProStart program work toward certification granted by the National Restaurant Association. Requirements for certification include passing an exam for each of the two years of the program, as well as completing four hundred hours of on-the-job training.

Bartenders

Bartenders serve drinks, both alcoholic and nonalcoholic. That may involve mixing drinks or pouring drinks into glasses using carbonated beverage dispensers. Bartenders may serve customers directly or give drinks to waiters and waitresses to serve.

Job Duties

The primary duty of bartenders is to mix, pour, and serve alcoholic and nonalcoholic drinks. They also check people's identification to make sure that they are of legal age to consume alcohol. Taking payment for drinks and ensuring that their work area is clean are also part of bartending duties. Bartenders order supplies and make sure that the bar is fully stocked.

Unofficially, bartenders are ambassadors who represent the place where they work. They greet customers when they come in the door or step up to the bar, keep customers happy and comfortable when they have to wait for tables, and traditionally lend a sympathetic ear to customers who want to talk about their day or their life.

Work Environment

Bartenders work at restaurants, bars, clubs, hotels, and other places where food is served. Some work full-time. Most work evenings, weekends, and holidays. The work can be stressful during busy hours. Bartenders also have to make sure that alcoholic beverages aren't served to minors.

Education and Training

There are no specific education requirements to become a bartender. Most of the training takes place on the job. Higher-end restaurants may prefer bartenders who have experience at other places. Because they serve alcohol, bartenders have to meet age requirements. Some states allow those who are at least eighteen years old to mix and serve alcohol, while others look for workers who are twenty-five or older.

While there are no formal education requirements to pursue a career as a bartender, training classes offered by trade schools can help high school graduates gain that all-important first job in the business. Training in one's field of choice shows that a person is serious about his or her career, and it may help the employee when promotion time comes around.

Trade school programs include classes on mixology (the mixing of alcohol to make certain drinks), garnishing glasses, and proper dress and behavior when behind the bar. Rules and regulations pertaining to serving alcoholic beverages in the state and local areas where the school is located are also covered.

Chapter Two

A COMFORTABLE STAY

A hotel's staff is in charge of making guests feel at home—or even more pampered than they might be at home. They work together to give customers a good experience when they travel. The comfort and safety of guests, in one form or another, is the responsibility of all hotel staffers.

Hotel jobs can be broken down by the various departments in which people work. The people who check guests in and out are considered front desk workers. Employees who clean and prepare rooms are referred to as housekeeping.

Concierge

When guests have questions about nearby restaurants or want to book a sightseeing tour, they visit the hotel's concierge. A concierge's job varies depending on the place where he or she works. In luxury hotels, at resorts, on cruise ships, or even in high-end apartment buildings, a concierge is like a butler who fulfills any request that a guest might make. Concierges

Hotel guests visit the concierge's desk to get directions, restaurant recommendations, and taxi cabs, among other reasons. Concierges make sure guests feel comfortable at the hotel.

also work in private residences, assisting clients with day-to-day activities. Some work in hospitals, helping patients take care of personal needs.

Job Duties

A concierge's job description seems pretty simple: help guests enjoy their stay at a hotel. In practice, this is

"KEEPER OF THE CANDLES"

The term "concierge" comes from the French *comte des cierges*, which means "keeper of the candles." In medieval times, this person was a servant in noble houses of France who was responsible for heating and lighting the house. Over time, the role expanded to providing an overall comfortable life to French nobility.

quite complex because of all the ways that the concierge can make that happen. Each guest has different needs, and it's up to the concierge to be flexible enough to meet every request.

Hotel concierges are jacks-of-all-trades, meaning that they have a lot of information about a variety of subjects. They know all about hotel policy and procedures and how to get things done within the hotel's walls. More than that, they must also have complete, up-to-date information about the area surrounding the hotel.

Concierges give recommendations about restaurants, entertainment venues, and events taking place near the hotel. They are very familiar with the lay of the land because they frequently give guests directions to locations within a city or on the outskirts of town. Concierges make dinner and spa reservations, and they may even go so far as to set up a tour for visitors. They can arrange to get specialty items (food, medication) or things that guests forgot to pack.

Finally, concierges assist with guest transportation needs. This includes just about anything, from arranging for ground transportation like taxis and shuttles to calling an airline on a guest's day of departure to see if his or her flight is on time.

Work Environment

A concierge works directly with customers, so a person interested in this occupation needs to have strong people skills. A concierge has to always be polite and present a professional image. Concierges must also

HOSPITALITY IN THE ER

A trend has emerged in concierge services. Hospitals are hiring concierges to help patients with everything from moving a parked car to finding care for a pet or filling a prescription after they've left the hospital. Some hospitals hire their own concierges, while others contract with a company that provides the service. The service allows families to stay with their loved ones instead of running errands.

be familiar with the area and be resourceful. If they don't know how to meet a client's request, they will have to figure it out in a timely manner. This could involve making several phone calls or doing Internet searches to find the answer. A concierge must be organized. He or she will likely handle multiple customer requests at a time.

Concierges may work alone or be part of a team. Those who work alone have to be independent. Those who work on teams need to be good communicators to keep the entire team up to date on requests.

Concierges may work full-time or part-time. Because hotels are open twenty-four hours a day, some concierges may have to work overnight, in the evening, and on the weekend.

Education and Training

Most employers require candidates for concierge jobs to have a high school diploma, but no formal education beyond that is required. Some vocational education programs in hospitality have courses or training of some sort for being a concierge, and some enterprising folks have created programs that give certification in concierge duties. Many hotels prefer to offer on-the-job training instead.

Preparation for a job as a concierge can begin in high school. Students can take communication classes, which should help them in this very people-oriented position. Seeking an internship at a hotel that would most likely include experience in many different positions, including concierge, would also be helpful.

Front Desk Clerks

Often the first person a guest sees at a hotel is the front desk clerk. This is the person who checks guests in and out, assigns rooms, hands out keys, and accepts payment for a guest's stay. At many smaller hotels and motels, the front desk clerk also takes reservations.

Job Duties

The first job of every desk clerk is to greet guests. The whole concept behind hospitality is making guests feel welcome and comfortable.

Next, front desk clerks are responsible for checking guests in and getting them into a room as quickly and conveniently as possible. People are tired after traveling to a

A hotel desk clerk hands a guest a room key card. Front desk clerks assist guests when they are checking in and out of hotels.

hotel or resort, and all they want to do is get into their room to rest and unpack. Front desk clerks check to see if guests have a reservation, and if not, they must figure out what rooms may be available beyond those reserved for other guests. Also, before handing a room key to a guest, they must make sure that the room has been cleaned and well stocked with towels, blankets, soap, and other amenities.

Front desk personnel answer phones and take messages for guests. They may also take reservations or connect callers to a reservation agent.

The person at the front desk acts as a cashier of sorts, accepting payment from guests at the end of their stay. Part of their job description calls for them to ask if guests had a nice stay and take suggestions for hotel operations that guests think need improvement. Of course, they also get to hear lots of compliments about the way the hotel is run.

Work Environment

A hotel clerk must have strong people skills and be willing to work directly with customers. Hotel clerks stand for long periods of time. They may need to help many guests at once, so the job can be stressful. Hotel clerks work around the clock, on weekends, and on holidays.

Education and Training

Typically, hotel clerks are trained on the job. Most hotels prefer to hire people with a high school diploma, but an associate's or bachelor's degree in hospitality or business certainly increases a person's chances of being hired. An advanced degree or vo-tech certification in hospitality would also come in handy if a front desk clerk is looking to be promoted to the hotel's business office or a management position on the desk staff. Hospitality and tourism vocational training programs most likely offer courses in front desk work.

Hotel clerks need to know computer basics to register guests, so computer and keyboarding skills are helpful. These are skills that students can pick up in high school.

Housekeeping

Housekeeping staff are in charge of keeping hotels, restaurants, resorts, homes, nursing homes, and hospitals clean. Depending on where they work, they may have other duties as well. For example, a person who works in a private home may be responsible for picking up dry-cleaning and running errands. A person who works in a hospital may have to disinfect medical equipment. Hotel housekeeping staff may deliver items, such as cribs, to guest rooms.

Job Duties

Making sure that the rooms and common areas of a hotel are clean and operational is the main duty of housekeeping staff. These employees vacuum, dust, scrub bathrooms, wash floors, change sheets, and

A housekeepr, or room attendant, finishes making the bed in a hotel room. The housekeeping staff makes sure rooms are clean and ready for guests.

stock rooms with items like clean towels and fresh toiletries (soap, shampoo, etc.). They also keep a running inventory of what they use in their daily jobs, loading carts with equipment and cleaning supplies at the start of each shift and reloading as necessary.

Work Environment

Most housekeeping employees work full-time, and more than a quarter are employed in hotels or motels. Others work in private households, hospitals, and service buildings. The work takes place inside, but it can be physically demanding. Housekeeping workers stand for long periods of time and may have to carry heavy equipment or lift mattresses and furniture.

Education and Training

Many duties of a housekeeper are tasks that students are familiar with while living at home. How the staff of a certain hotel might perform housekeeping duties is covered in training once a person is hired. New employees may work with experienced employees for a short time before striking out on their own.

There are no formal education requirements. These employees have to be detail-oriented and have strong communication skills, since they will be working with customers. They also need stamina because the work can be physically demanding.

Bellhop

Bellhops are employed by hotels, motels, resorts, and airports to carry luggage. They are also called baggage handlers. A bellhop may also hail a cab for a visitor, open doors, and help visitors check out of the hotel. The term comes from "bellhopper," a person who was called by guests ringing a bell to get service. The duties of a bellhop vary depending on the place of employment, but all bellhops need strong customer service skills.

Job Duties

Following is a brief breakdown of the day-to-day activities of a bellhop:

- Haul luggage from a vehicle to a hotel room and from a hotel room to the lobby or vehicle
- Greet guests
- Open doors

Work Environment

Most bellhops work in hotels or motels. Bellhops stand for long periods of time and carry luggage, so it is physical labor.

Education and Training

As one might imagine, there are no formal education requirements to be a bellhop. After all, people don't

Bellhops or baggage handlers assist guests with their luggage. Students interested in the hospitality field may start in this position while they are still in high school.

need training in how to open doors and carry luggage. However, being a bellhop might be an entry-level job that someone takes to work his or her way up to another position within a hotel. Vocational training in the hospitality field might not be a bad idea for high school students with a rising career path in mind. If not, then taking courses that sharpen one's interpersonal skills, as well as physical fitness training to increase stamina, would be steps one could take while still in high school.

Chapter Three

MANAGING IT ALL

Overseeing the work of hospitality employees of every stripe are various managers. Unlike the many entry-level positions to be found in the hospitality and tourism field, managers generally are expected to have some kind of college degree. However, some employers might be willing to take a chance on someone with vocational training coupled with a few years of experience in a hospitality job, particularly if the job experience took place within their own establishment.

Lodging Managers

Lodging managers run hotels, resorts, and other places where people stay. They are the people who make sure that customers have a good experience and want to return when they visit the area again. Some lodging managers are in charge of small inns with just a few rooms. Others run large hotels with hundreds of rooms and several restaurants on-site.

Lodging managers oversee hotel and resort operations. As part of their job, managers should be friendly and work well with others, both staff and customers.

Lodging managers also run hotels with casinos or hotels that host large conferences.

There are several types of lodging managers. General managers oversee lodging operations, including the work of assistant managers who run departments, such as housekeeping, security, food services, maintenance, and recreational facilities. Revenue managers oversee accounting activities and keep track of finances, which can include deciding when to offer special rates. Front office managers coordinate reservations and room assignments and supervise the hotel's front desk staff. Convention service managers coordinate meetings and special events at the facility, including assigning conference rooms, setting up meeting spaces, and coordinating equipment for meetings.

Job Duties

Managers oversee a lot, so their job duties are multiple and varied. Lodging managers are responsible for making sure that everyone on the hotel or resort staff does his or her job properly. Therefore, they are ultimately responsible for greeting guests, as front desk clerks would; making sure that all areas of the hotel or resort are clean and tidy, which is the job done by housekeeping; ensuring that visits to restaurants and entertainment venues, staffed by chefs, servers, and performers hired by the hotel or resort, are pleasant for guests; and being on-hand to settle billing disputes or other problems encountered by guests.

Another major aspect of a lodging manager's job involves personnel matters, such as hiring, firing, and training. These hospitality employees also create work schedules for their staff and monitor individual performance on the job. They order supplies and keep track of inventory; they do it themselves or oversee the staff who accomplish these tasks.

Work Environment

Most lodging managers work in hotels and motels. Others work at youth hostels, inns, boardinghouses, bed and breakfasts, resorts, and summer camps. The job can be stressful. Lodging managers have to work with guests, coordinate activities, and make a profit. Most work full-time. Some may work weekends and holidays because hotels are open around the clock. Some are on call twenty-four hours a day to handle problems.

Education and Training

Some lodging managers may have only a high school diploma and some related work experience, but most hotels and resorts require job candidates for this position to have a four-year degree. Smaller hotels may hire managers with an associate's degree or a certificate in hotel or hospitality management. The Accreditation Commission for Programs in Hospitality Administration (ACPHA) accredits hospitality management programs across the country.

Some high schools offer lodging management programs, including those offered through the American

Pictured here are winners of the hotel management division of the 2013 Concours General, a competition for French high school students. Preparation for a lodging management career can begin in high school.

Hotel and Lodging Educational Institute (AHLEI) in the United States. High school juniors and seniors interested in this career can learn lodging management, front office management, leadership skills, and marketing and sales skills in this program. They also get the opportunity to get real work experience. Students who complete the program earn a certification called Certified Rooms Division Executive (CRDE).

Some places are streamlining operations to save money. Hotel chains may hire a single manager to oversee multiple hotels. People with a college degree have the best opportunities for jobs.

Food Service Managers

Food service managers oversee restaurants and other places that serve food and beverages. They make sure that customers have a good experience and want to return. They oversee health and safety guidelines and standards set by the restaurant. They create the schedule and may even fill in for other positions when staffing is short. Managers also keep track of employee records, prepare the payroll, and complete paperwork to comply with local, state, and national laws. Larger restaurants may have a management team that includes the food service manager, assistant managers, and an executive chef.

Job Duties

Like lodging managers, food service managers oversee many activities. They hire and train employees, order supplies, make schedules, evaluate staff performance, handle payments, and enforce rules. Since they are at the top level of their staff, food service managers are also the ones who field customer complaints and resolve issues stemming from the service at their restaurants.

Because their employees handle food, these managers must make sure that health and safety codes are adhered to at all times. Some work closely with chefs to create exciting and tasty menus.

Work Environment

Food service managers work in all types of restaurants, from fine-dining establishments to fast-food chains. They also work in cafeterias in schools, hospitals, offices, universities, and factories.

A restaurant manager reviews the day's menu with a waitress. Food service managers oversee every aspect of a well-run professional kitchen.

Most food service managers work full-time, and long hours are typical. Managers who work in schools and offices have more regular hours than those who work at restaurants that are open late seven days a week. The job is stressful because managers are responsible for resolving customer complaints.

Education and Training

Many food service managers get their start as cooks, waiters, or waitresses. However, some places of employment want managers who have received an education beyond a high school diploma. In fact, applicants with a degree typically have an advantage when competing for jobs at upscale restaurants.

A number of community colleges offer associate's degrees and certification in the areas of restaurant and hospitality management or institutional food service management. Through these programs, students take classes in nutrition, sanitation, food planning, and preparation, as well as some business courses. Some programs require internships through which students can get on-the-job training.

Meeting, Convention, and Event Planners

Meeting, convention, and event planners are the equivalent of a manager because everything that goes into a successful meeting or event is part of their job. They coordinate professional meetings and events, such as weddings. They pick the location for the meeting, organize transportation for participants, coordinate meals, and handle all other details from the beginning to the end. On the day of the event, they make sure that everything goes as planned.

Association planners organize annual conferences and trade shows for professional organizations. Corporate planners organize business meetings, while convention service managers organize larger events for hotels and convention centers. Personal events, such as weddings and parties, are pulled together by people simply known as event planners.

AT THE WHIM OF THE ECONOMY

According to the *Occupational Outlook Handbook*, the future for event planners looks pretty good. As the scope of businesses becomes more international, the need for people who can pull off successful meetings and conventions on a large scale and in distant locations will most likely grow along with it. However, job opportunities for meeting, convention, and event planners change with the economy. When the economy is bad, some corporate planners may lose their jobs. Planners in the health care industry are least likely to be affected by the economy.

Job Duties

Meeting, convention, and event planners start each job by meeting with clients in order to understand the purpose of the event or meeting, as well as what the clients' expectations are. Once they have the particulars in place, they start on the nitty-gritty of planning the event. This includes inspecting and booking a site,

Meeting, convention, and event planners have to pay attention to details. They are responsible for making sure an event goes the way a client expects it to.

asking for and reviewing bids from service providers, hiring staff, negotiating contracts, and coordinating the work of many different service providers.

Planners don't just set up events and meetings. They have work to do after the event as well. Consulting with clients post-event lets them know what went well and what went not so well so that they can make amends (fix things) and make note of trouble spots to avoid in the future. Then there is the matter of getting paid. Planners review all bills for services provided with the client, as well as discuss their own payment for coordinating everything. Follow-up paperwork, including correspondence (letters, e-mail messages) and invoices, is also the responsibility of meeting, convention, and event planners.

Work Environment

Planners work in offices except during meetings and events, when they are at hotels or convention centers. They travel to attend the events that they organize and visit possible meeting sites.

Education and Training

Employers prefer applicants who have a college degree in planning or hospitality management. However, vocational training is available in some areas for people who have professional planning experience. For instance, the Convention Industry Council (CIC), a professional association in the planning field, offers a voluntary certification for meeting and convention planners. To qualify, candidates need to have at least three years of meeting management experience and pass an exam.

The Society of Government Meeting Professionals (SGMP) offers the Certified Government Meeting Professional (CGMP) certification for meeting planners who work for or contract with federal, state, or local government. To qualify, candidates need to have worked as a meeting planner for at least one year and pass an exam.

Chapter Four

BY AIR OR BY SEA

Hospitality and tourism cannot, and should not, be grounded. A number of career positions in this field take employees out of cities and towns and put them to work flying through the sky or sailing on waves and swells. Some of the most recognizable of these jobs include airline flight attendant and cruise ship director. Then there are the workers who are on land most of the time but may take advantage of air and sea travel as part of their jobs: travel agents.

Travel Agents

Travel agents arrange trips, including transportation to and from a destination, lodging, and admission to entertainment activities. This usually means investigating all possible options, location- and pricewise, and helping clients select the best travel package for them.

Travel agents may travel themselves and visit destinations so that they can make recommendations to clients. They visit restaurants and hotels to determine if they want to recommend those places.

Some work on only one type of travel, such as Disney vacations. Some may work only with specific groups, such as businesses or single people. Some travel agents work for tour companies and sell the company's tour packages.

A worker in a California student travel agency helps a customer book a trip. Travel agents arrange transportation, lodging, and on-location activities. They also help solve problems during the trip.

Job Duties

Travel agents can be described as people who spend hours, days, or even weeks planning the perfect vacation or trip—and then sending others off to enjoy the fruits of their labor. They take everything into account, from arranging transportation to and from a destination, accommodations (hotel rooms, rentals, etc.) while clients are away from home, and even tours or day trips.

Travel agents consult with clients—either in person or by phone or e-mail—to find out where people need or want to go. If someone doesn't know exactly where to vacation, travel agents are ready with suggestions based on a client's personality and budget. They collect all tickets and other paperwork that travelers need and present them to clients for use on their journey. They also make themselves available to help clients make new travel arrangements if changes need to be made before or during a trip.

Work Environment

Travel agents work in offices. They spend time on the phone with clients and on the computer booking trips. The job can be stressful if a client has a travel emergency or an unexpected schedule change. Most travel agents work full-time.

Education and Training

Travel agents need a high school diploma to get started. Employers prefer people who know something about

MAKING A COMEBACK

In the age of online sites such as Travelocity, Kayak, and TripAdvisor, the role of the travel agent has not been as strong or seemingly necessary as it once was. As a 2012 article in *Time* magazine noted, the number of physical travel agencies has declined greatly since the 1990s; the amount of booking through existing agencies has declined as well. This is the result of a do-it-yourself mentality, where travelers book trips themselves.

The *Time* article noted, however, that travel agencies are making a comeback. Many personal travelers have turned to travel agents to find and schedule great deals on trips because doing so themselves is often too confusing and time-consuming. Because they likely have special contacts not available to "wholesale" travel sites, travel agents are able to offer special deals, such as a discounted tour or reservations at an exclusive restaurant. All this and more explains why being a travel agent is a career on the upswing.

the travel industry. Community colleges and vocational schools offer classes in professional travel planning. Some employers supplement formal schooling or training with on-the-job training.

The Travel Institute offers a Certified Travel Associate (CTA) certification. The program leading up to such certification helps participants sharpen their customer service and communication skills. People need to complete twelve Travel Institute courses and log at least eighteen months of work experience as a travel agent to qualify for the CTA.

Those who have a CTA certificate and five additional years of experience in the field can enroll in the organization's Certified Travel Counselor (CTC) program. In addition to taking courses on general topics such as business planning and financial planning, CTC candidates can major in marketing, management, sales and customer relationships, communication, or personal development. Submission of a white paper, which is a report on a particular area of the travel and tourism field, is the final requirement for CTC certification.

Some states require travel agents to have a business license before they can sell travel services.

Flight Attendants

Once the reservations have been made, other people make sure that travelers have a good trip. At the airport, ticketing staff are usually the first people to greet customers. Many of these jobs are entry-level, but they require good communication skills. A high school diploma is typically required. Ticketing agents check in baggage, advise travelers, help rebook when flights are canceled or delayed, and solve problems.

Once passengers are in the air, however, they are in the care of flight attendants, who make sure that

Flight attendants make sure passengers are comfortable and safe while traveling by air. They may work for commercial airlines or private companies.

the airline's customers are safe and comfortable. Flight attendants instruct passengers on safety procedures before the flight takes off. They make sure that equipment is working, baggage is stored properly, and passengers are wearing their seat belts. Their most important role is to help passengers during an emergency. This means keeping passengers calm, giving them first aid, and evacuating them if necessary.

Job Duties

Flight attendants greet fliers as they enter the plane, helping them find their seats and stow any carry-on luggage. Other responsibilities with regard to customers include serving refreshments, answering questions, making announcements, and making sure that fliers stay safe on takeoff and landing, as well as while in the air.

Before takeoff, flight attendants are responsible for preparing for the flight. This includes making sure that the plane has enough refreshments and appropriate emergency equipment and that the equipment is in working order.

Work Environment

Flight attendants work in the cabin of an airplane. They stand during most of the flight, and they must stay calm and remain pleasant. Most work for airline companies. Some work for corporations or chartered flight companies.

According to the *Occupational Outlook Handbook*, flight attendants have more work-related injuries and illnesses than the average worker. They may also experience medical problems from irregular sleep patterns, stress, and working in a pressurized cabin. Most work an irregular schedule, weekends, and holidays. A typical shift is about twelve to fourteen hours a day. The Federal Aviation Administration (FAA) requires that flight attendants receive nine consecutive hours of rest following any duty period.

Attendants fly between seventy-five and ninety hours a month and spend another fifty hours a month on the ground preparing flights. On average, they spend two to three nights a week away from home. Generally, a flight attendant is assigned routes based on seniority, which means new flight attendants need to be flexible. The more seniority flight attendants have, the more control they have over their schedules.

Education and Training

In addition to having earned their high school diploma or GED, people who want to work as flight attendants must be certified by the FAA. Before receiving this certification, prospective flight attendants need to get training, which is offered by aviation training facilities as well as some colleges. Once they have passed this initial training, flight attendants get the FAA Certificate of Demonstrated Proficiency. In order to keep the certification, they have to complete periodic training throughout their careers. Besides formal training, most airlines also train flight attendants on emergency procedures, flight regulations, and other job duties.

Airlines prefer to hire people with a college degree in hospitality, tourism, public relations, or communications, and they would like applicants to have one to two years of customer service experience. Applicants need to have a valid passport and undergo a background check.

Cruise Directors

Cruise directors make sure that all guests aboard a cruise ship have fun. They essentially manage the social part of a cruise and may oversee staff. They plan events, offer support to guests, and encourage guests to participate. They are cheerleaders and problem solvers.

Job Duties

The following is a brief breakdown of the day-to-day activities of a cruise director:

- Greet guests when they arrive
- Plan activities for all ages
- Supervise other hospitality workers aboard the ship
- Oversee the entertainment on the ship, which could include musicians, actors, stage managers, and staff
- Communicate with the dining crew, captain, and hospitality crew to keep things on schedule

ALL ABOARD!

Cruise ships offer something for everyone, from gourmet buffets and contests to live shows and music, to dancing and exercise. Because there are so many activities on board, there also are many jobs on cruise ships as well. In addition to cruise ship directors, there are sales associates who staff gift shops and other retail outlets. Medical personnel are on board to care for anyone who is injured or ill while the ship is out to sea. Pursers manage accounts and excursions. There are staff photographers and videographers, as well as performers who entertain passengers on their voyage.

- Take on the role of master of ceremonies for big events on the ship
- Order props
- Complete clerical work, such as schedules, employee reviews, and evaluations
- Budget and bill for entertainment
- Offer support to guests and make sure that guests are having a good time

Work Environment

Cruise directors interact with hundreds of people in a given day, so they must be good communicators and be able to multitask. The job is not nine-to-five.

A cruise director introduces fellow crew members from a ship's stage, combining his duties as a master of ceremonies and head of the ship's hospitality crew.

Cruises can last many days, so the workweek is long. Cruise directors are always on call, and it can be stressful handling customer complaints.

Education and Training

Experience trumps a formal education or training when trying to get a job as a cruise director. Many first work in hotels or restaurants. Starting as an entertainer, server, or assistant cruise director, most people in this position work their way up the career ladder. Working beside an experienced cruise director is also a tactic that has served beginning cruise ship workers well.

Some cruise lines hold their own vocational training. Skills that are taught in these employer-offered training programs include how to deal with difficult passengers, create and adapt a schedule, and even administer minor first aid and CPR.

A secondary education gives candidates an advantage, particularly those who have taken courses in business, management, or hospitality.

Chapter Five

A JOB AND AN ADVENTURE

A new type of vacation has emerged where people travel to natural areas to better understand the environment. This is called ecotourism. Travelers not only get to see new areas, but they also help support the conservation efforts of those locations. According to the International Ecotourism Society (TIES), ecotourism is responsible travel to natural areas that conserves the environment and improves the well-being of local people. In other words, ecotourists work hard not to leave a footprint on a place that they visit and, if anything, leave the place in better condition than when they arrived.

For those who like the idea of helping others have fun but prefer to remain close to home, there is the option of landing a job as a recreation worker.

Ecotourism Positions

Ecotourism helps preserve cultural traditions and protect sacred sites around the world. Leading the way in this new and growing field are professionals whose job it is to make sure that clients enjoy their travels and adventures and learn a bit about the fragile environments they visit, as well as ensuring that the delicate ecobalance of a location remains intact. People who perform these tasks are known as ecotourism coordinators or ecotourism guides.

A tour guide explains aboriginal paintings in Australia's Kakadu National Park. Sharing yet protecting such sensitive cultural and natural sites is the main focus of an ecotourism guide's job.

Job Duties

Ecotourism coordinators are like travel agents in that they help arrange ecotours for travelers. They develop an itinerary, book airfare, arrange lodging, and develop activities that benefit the local community. Ecotourism guides educate tourists about the region and local issues. Naturalists, conservationists, and anthropologists are likely to snag jobs in the ecotourism industry.

Work Environment

Ecotourism employees can work for a government, private tourism company, or nongovernmental organization.

PITCHING IN ON VACATION

A study conducted by Conservation International (CI) has indicated that tourism in the great outdoors has increased greatly since the 1990s. Unfortunately, some of the most popular spots for visitors also happen to be home to unique, protected animals and plants. Ecotourism helps keep these spots from being ruined by human activity.

Certain types of ecotours can do more, however, by getting tourists involved in conservation activities. For instance, some ecotourism companies feature tours where travelers may not just observe how animals behave but also actively help map where exotic animals live.

The positions generally involve working outdoors. The hours can be long, depending on the position. A lot of this type of work takes place outdoors, possibly in locations that are remote and, because such tours are ecologically friendly and therefore in a natural state, without a lot of amenities, such as restaurants, gift shops, or even restrooms.

Education and Training

Ecotourism employees need to understand the area in which they are working so that they can help clients find lodging and work opportunities. Employees need to understand sustainable development, ecological business management, natural resources, and conservation issues. Employers prefer candidates with a bachelor's degree. Most employees receive on-the-job training.

Recreation Workers

Do you remember your favorite summer camp as a young child? Maybe it was an outdoor camp with a range of activities, from rope courses to arts and crafts. Or maybe it was a sports camp, focused on one activity like soccer. Recreation workers are the people who lead these group activities. They work at recreation facilities, such as playgrounds and parks. They work at summer camps and senior centers.

Many positions fall under the heading of "recreation worker." Among them are camp counselors, camp directors, activity specialists, recreation specialists, recreation leaders, and parks and recreation directors.

Camp counselors work at day camps and overnight camps. They lead campers in outdoor activities, such as swimming, hiking, and camping. Counselors who work at overnight camps also supervise daily living. They make sure that campers get enough sleep, shower, and eat properly.

A counselor (*far right*) teaches campers about safe kayaking at a summer camp session. Camp counselors—indeed, recreation workers in general—are considered hospitality workers.

Camp directors supervise camp counselors. They plan activities and programs and perform administrative tasks.

Activity specialists teach specialized areas, such as archery, rope courses, sailing, music, tennis, or drama. These specialists may work at overnight camps, day camps, or camps focused on that activity.

Recreation leaders are responsible for a recreation program's daily operation. They organize and direct participants, schedule the use of facilities, keep records of equipment use, and make sure that participants are using equipment properly.

Recreation supervisors oversee recreation leaders. They are the people between the director of a park or recreation center and the recreation leaders. They plan activities and may oversee special activities or events.

The directors of parks and recreation develop and manage recreation programs in municipal parks and playgrounds. They may oversee a park budget and work with state or local recreation and park commissions.

Job Duties

No matter what level of job they hold, recreation workers are basically responsible for the happiness and relaxation of others. They plan fun and educational activities for groups of people, large and small, or individuals. Ordering any equipment or tools necessary to make sure that these activities go smoothly is part of their job description. Recreation workers enforce safety guidelines to prevent injuries, and they administer first aid when injuries do occur.

Professionals in this career field must be flexible. They need to be ready to modify activities in order to fit the needs of the group. For example, activities may be changed to better accommodate senior citizens or people with disabilities.

Work Environment

Recreation workers can be found in many different settings. They work at summer camps and recreation centers and in parks and on cruise ships. Many spend much of their workday outside. Recreation directors and supervisors spend more time in an office planning programs. Some recreation workers, such as camp counselors, work long irregular hours. Their work is also seasonal.

Some recreation workers specialize in and teach a specific sport such as tennis or sailing.

Education and Training

Many recreation workers have a college education,

but a degree is not required for this type of work. Most seasonal and part-time workers learn on the job. Those who work in a specialized area, such as art or athletics, need experience and training in their area of expertise.

A bachelor's degree is helpful for full-time workers. Some supervisory or administrative positions in this field require that applicants have at least a bachelor's degree, if not a master's degree, in business administration or public administration. College students interested in this field should take courses in management, community organization, supervision, and administration. They may also specialize in areas such as park management or camp management.

Along with education, all of these workers need to be mature, have experience leading activities, and be able to work well with children and the elderly. They need to make sure that participants stay safe.

Generally, job prospects are best for those seeking part-time or seasonal jobs, such as camp counselors. Most of these workers are young people who need to be replaced when they finish school and go on to other jobs. Those with higher levels of education will have the best opportunity to get a full-time position.

Outdoor Adventure Guides

Outdoor adventure guides organize and lead trips for adventurers. They work for adventure tourism companies, resorts, parks, lodges, and campgrounds. They take tourists whitewater rafting, fishing, hunting, mountain climbing, and rock climbing.

Job Duties

Adventure guides take groups on expeditions in wilderness or untamed environments. As guides, they must know everything about the area that guests are visiting, including its history, and they must be able to communicate this knowledge to the group in an interesting manner. The clear and correct demonstration of certain activities and techniques related to the adventure they are leading is essential.

An adventure guide takes a family on safari in Kenya. There is more to an adventure guide's job than the adventure. Guides also do preparation and cleanup.

Not everything these guides do is a grand adventure. Setting up camp, assembling equipment, ordering supplies, cooking for the group, and filling out paperwork are all part of the adventure guide job experience, as well as the more thrilling stuff.

Work Environment

The work is generally seasonal and may be part-time or full-time. The job is for those who like to be outside and can handle the physical demands of carrying equipment.

Education and Training

Adventure guides will face many physical demands. They need to be trained in first aid and CPR. They also need good communication and leadership skills, and they must be able to work in teams. Previous experience in the activity is required. Some certification is required. For example, mountain guides must be accredited.

Some people enter this field because of their interest in an outdoor sport. People who want to pursue this occupation full-time should take college classes in tourism, outdoor education, and management.

Glossary

accredited Given official approval, usually granted by a trade or similar organization.

apprentice A person who is learning a trade or occupation by working with a more experienced person in that field.

certification Official recognition that someone has met all the requirements to perform a certain job or task.

concierge One whose job is to assist hotel guests by running errands, making reservations, and arranging tours.

ecotourism Tourism to exotic or threatened ecosystems to observe wildlife or help preserve nature.

executive chef The chief cook, responsible for planning menus, ordering food, overseeing food preparation, and supervising kitchen staff.

expedition A trip or journey taken by a group to a place far from home.

hospitality The relationship between the guest and the host. This includes the reception and entertainment of guests, visitors, or strangers.

housekeeping The care and cleaning of a property, such as a hotel.

internship A supervised work experience that may be paid or unpaid, typically performed by a student or recent graduate.

lodging A place where travelers stop and rest; also a hotel or motel.

municipal Owned or overseen by a local government.

sous chef The chef who is second in authority in a restaurant or kitchen, ranking below the head chef.

tourism The practice of traveling for recreation.

vocational Refers to special skills or training necessary to get a certain job or follow a particular career path.

For More Information

Accreditation Commission for Programs in Hospitality Administration (ACPHA)
P.O. Box 400
Oxford, MD 21654
(410) 226-5527
Website: http://www.acpha-cahm.org
The ACPHA evaluates hospitality education programs in the United States. Established in 1989, it consists of fourteen commissioners, including hospitality educators; executives from the lodging, restaurant, and hospitality industries; and member representatives from the travel industry.

American Culinary Federation (ACF)
180 Center Place Way
St. Augustine, FL 32095
(800) 624-9458
Website: http://www.acfchefs.org
The ACF is one of the premier professional chef organizations in North America, with more than twenty thousand members in more than two hundred chapters.

American Hotel & Lodging Educational Institute (AHLEI)
800 N. Magnolia Avenue, Suite 300
Orlando, FL 32803
(800) 344-4381
Website: http://www.ahlei.org
Founded in 1953 to educate and train hospitality professionals, the AHLEI provides those in the hospitality industry with online learning and professional certification, and it offers resources to high schools, colleges, and workforce agencies.

Canadian Restaurant and Foodservices Association
  (CRFA)
316 Bloor Street W.
Toronto, ON M5S 1W5
Canada
(800) 387-5649
Website: http://www.crfa.ca
Since its founding in 1944, the CRFA has grown to more
  than thirty thousand members across the country.
  Through advocacy, research, member savings, and
  industry events, the organization helps members in
  every Canadian community grow and prosper.

International Council on Hotel, Restaurant, and Institutional Education (CHRIE)
2810 North Parham Road, Suite 230
Richmond, VA 23294
(804) 346-4800
Website: http://www.chrie.org
Founded in 1946, the CHRIE is the global advocate of
  hospitality and tourism education for schools, colleges, and universities offering programs in hotel
  and restaurant management, food service management, and culinary arts.

The International Ecotourism Society (TIES)
P.O. Box 96503 #34145
Washington, DC 20090-6503
Website: http://www.ecotourism.org
TIES is a nonprofit organization dedicated to promoting
  ecotourism. Founded in 1990, it has been at the
  forefront of ecotourism development by providing

guidelines and standards, training, technical assistance, and educational resources.

National Restaurant Association (NRA)
2055 L Street NW, Suite 700
Washington, DC 20036
(800) 424-51566
Website: http://www.restaurant.org
The National Restaurant Association is among the largest food service trade associations in the world.

Retail Bakers of America (RBA)
15941 Harlem Avenue, #347
Tinley Park, IL 60477
(800) 638-0924
Website: http://www.retailbakersofamerica.org
Founded in 1918, the Retail Bakers of America is committed to the success of the retail baking industry. The organization is a baker's business partner connecting buyers and sellers to build profitable bakeries.

Websites

Due to the changing nature of Internet links, Rosen Publishing has developed an online list of websites related to the subject of this book. This site is updated regularly. Please use the following link to access the list:

http://www.rosenlinks.com/TRADE/Hosp

For Further Reading

Allen, Judy. *Event Planning: The Ultimate Guide to Successful Meetings, Corporate Events, Fundraising Galas, Conferences, Conventions, Incentives and Other Special Events*. Hoboken, NJ: Wiley, 2009.

Bedell, Jane. *So, You Want to Be a Chef?: How to Get Started in the World of Culinary Arts* (Be What You Want). Peabody, MA: Aladdin/Beyond Words, 2013.

Culinary Institute of America. *The Professional Chef*. Hoboken, NJ: Wiley, 2011.

Dakers, Diane. *Touring, Trekking, and Traveling Green: Careers in Ecotourism*. New York, NY: Crabtree Publishing, 2011.

Evans, Virginia, Jenny Dooley, and Veronica Garza. *Career Paths—Hotels & Catering: Student's Book*. Newbury, Berkshire, England: Express Publishing, 2011

Fiore, Kelly. *Taste Test*. New York, NY: Walker Books for Young Readers, 2013.

Gordon, Howard R. D. *The History and Growth of Career and Technical Education in America*. Lake Grove, IL: Waveland Press, 2008.

Hall, Kirsten, and Christian Schulz. *Hospitality* (Ferguson Career Launcher). New York, NY: Ferguson Publishing, 2010.

Institute for Career Research. *Career as a Chef*. Chicago, IL: Institute for Career Research, 2013.

Kitazawa, Yuko. *Career Diary of a Pastry Chef: Gardner's Guide Series*. Herndon, VA: Garth Gardner Company, 2008.

Kotler, Philip R., John T. Bowen, and James Makens. *Marketing for Hospitality & Tourism*. Upper Saddle River, NJ: Prentice Hall, 2009.

Meyer, Susan. *A Career as a Chef* (Essential Careers).
New York, NY: Rosen Publishing, 2012.

Nixon, James. *Chef* (What We Do). London, England:
Franklin Watts, 2012.

O'Fallon, Michael J., and Denney G. Rutherford. *Hotel
Management and Operations*. Hoboken, NJ: Wiley,
2010.

Senke, Cath. *Hospitality and Catering Careers* (In the
Workplace). Mankato, MN: Amicus, 2011.

Smilow, Rick, and Anne E. McBride. *Culinary Careers:
How to Get Your Dream Job in Food with Advice from
Top Culinary Professionals*. New York, NY: Clarkson
Potter, 2010.

Tanji, Hotelier. *170 Hotel Management Training Tutori-
als: Practical Training Guide for Professional Hote-
liers & Hospitality Students*. Seattle, WA: Create-
Space, 2012.

Vallen, Gary K., and Jerome J. Vallen. *Check-In Check-Out:
Managing Hotel Operations*. Upper Saddle River, NJ:
Prentice Hall, 2008.

Walsh, Andrew. *Made in Madagascar: Sapphires,
Ecotourism, and the Global Bazaar* (Teaching
Culture: UTP Ethnographies for the Classroom).
Toronto, Canada: University of Toronto Press, 2012.

Bibliography

Austin, Anne. "Hot Jobs in Hospitality." *Career World*, October 2002. Retrieved January 2014 (http://elibrary.bigchalk.com/k6).

Barchenger, Stacey. "Who's Working on the Cruise Ships You're Sailing Aboard?" *USA Today*, June 6, 2013. Retrieved August 8, 2013 (http://www.usa-today.com/story/travel/news/2013/06/10/cruise-ship-crew-background-checks/2407611).

Bryner, Jenna. "Eco-Tourism: Life." *Scholastic*, February 2, 2004. Vol. 60, no. 8/9, p. 11.

Buckley, Ralf. *Ecotourism Principles & Practices*. Wallingford, England: CAB International, 2009.

Bureau of Labor Statistics, U.S. Department of Labor. *Occupational Outlook Handbook*. 2012–13 ed. Retrieved August 2013 (http://www.bls.gov/ooh).

Culinary Institute of America. "Academics." Retrieved January 2014 (http://www.ciachef.edu/academics).

Dador, Denise. "Hospitals Now Offering Concierge Service." KABC-TV Los Angeles, July 31, 2009. Retrieved August 5, 2013 (http://abclocal.go.com/kabc/story?section=news/health&id=6943052).

Go2 Tourism HR Society. "Outdoor Adventure Guide." Retrieved August 6, 2013 (http://www.go2hr.ca/careers/outdoor-adventure-guide).

Higgins, Michelle. "Are Travel Agents Back?" *Time*, April 2012. Retrieved January 2014 (http://www.nytimes.com/2012/04/22/travel/are-travel-agents-back.html?_r=0).

Jacoby, Tamar. "College Isn't for Everyone." *Los Angeles Times*, December 3, 2013, A17.

Keedle, Jayne. "Wish You Were Here!" *Career World*, February 2008, Vol. 36, p. 21.

Levesque, Dawn R. "Examples of Ecotourism." *USA
  Today*. Retrieved August 9, 2013 (http://traveltips
  .usatoday.com/examples-ecotourism-18970.html).
Melandra, Ocean. "Definition of Ecotourism." *USA
  Today*. Retrieved August 9, 2013 (http://traveltips
  .usatoday.com/definition-ecotourism-10981.html).
National Restaurant Association. "Meet ProStart:
  Feeding Dreams, Building Futures." Retrieved
  January 2014 (http://www.nraef.org/ProStart).
Pascarella, Sarah. "What Can a Concierge Do for
  You?" *Smarter Travel*, April 6, 2010. Retrieved
  August 5, 2013 (http://www.smartertravel.com/
  travel-advice/what-can-concierge-do-for-you.html
  ?id=4851880).
Travel Institute. "Earn a Professional Certification."
  Retrieved January 2014 (http://thetravelinstitute
  .com/certification).
Trejos, Nancy. "Not All Travelers Want to Be Their Own
  Travel Agents; Many Prefer Human Help." *USA Today*,
  January 6, 2014, B4.
U.S. Department of Labor. "Specific Vocational
  Education." O*Net Online. Retrieved January 2014
  (http://www.onetonline.org/help/online/svp).

Index

About the Author

Mindy Mozer is a writer and editor living in Rochester, New York, with her husband and two children. *Getting a Job in Automotive Care and Service* and *Careers as a Commissioned Sales Representative* are among the other career-related titles that Mozer has written for Rosen Publishing.

Photo Credits

Cover (figure) Dean Drobot/Shutterstock.com; cover (background), pp. 1, 3 Photographee.eu/Shutterstock.com; p. 5 Kzenon/Shutterstock.com; p. 8 michaeljung/Shutterstock.com; p. 11 © AP Images; p. 15 Peter Dazeley/Photodisc/Getty Images; p. 19 webphotographeer/E+/Getty Images; p. 24 Comstock/Stockbyte/Thinkstock; pp. 28–29 racom/Shutterstock.com; p. 32 Robert Kneschke/Shutterstock.com; p. 35 Andrea Chu/Digital Vision/Thinkstock; p. 38 Glow Images, Inc./Getty Images; p. 41 Jacques Demarthon/AFP/Getty Images; p. 43 Anderson Ross/Photodisc/Getty Images; p. 46 Jetta Productions/Blend Images/Getty Images; p. 50 © Kayte Deioma/PhotoEdit; p. 54 B2M Productions/Photographer's Choice RF/Getty Images; p. 59 © Buskirk Services, Inc./PhotoEdit; p 62 Andrew Watson/Photolibrary/Getty Images; p. 65 kali9/iStock/Thinkstock; p. 67 Assembly/The Image Bank/Getty Images; p. 69 John Warburton-Lee/AWL Images/Getty Images; cover and interior elements joesayhello/Shutterstock.com (appetizers), Jirsak/ Shutterstock.com (tablet frame), schab/Shutterstock.com (text highlighting), nikifiva/ Shutterstock.com (stripe textures), Zfoto/Shutterstock.com (abstract curves); back cover graphics ramcreations/Shutterstock.com, vectorlib.com/Shutterstock.com (globe icon).

Designer: Michael Moy; Editor: Jeanne Nagle;
Photo Researcher: Karen Huang